Tile Style for the Home

Kitchens, Baths, and More

Tina Skinner, with the
Association of Ceramic Tile Manufacturers of Spain

Schiffer Publishing Ltd
4880 Lower Valley Road Atglen, Pennsylvania 19310

This book is made possible by the Association of Ceramic Tile Manufacturers of Spain (ASCER). Spain leads the world in wall tile production, shares the lead in global tile production, and produces a third of the world's tile exports. The U.S. is its top export market, where it continues to actively build the Tile of Spain brand in the commercial and residential marketplaces. Tile of Spain is the recognized brand for Spain's ceramic tile industry. Comprising 220 member manufacturers, ASCER is a private organization whose primary objective is to support Spain's ceramic tile manufacturers and the industry as a whole. To learn more, visit spaintiles.com.

Moreover, this book came about because of a dynamic firm, White Good & Co. Advertising, public relations representatives to ASCER. Staff members opened up their wonderful archives in order to bring this incredible book to life. See more about them at www.whitegood.com.

Copyright © 2007 by Schiffer Publishing, Ltd.
Library of Congress Control Number: 2007930645

Type set in Exotc350 Bd BT/Zurich BT

ISBN: 978- 0-7643-2773-5
Printed in China

Published by Schiffer Publishing Ltd.
4880 Lower Valley Road
Atglen, PA 19310
Phone: (610) 593-1777; Fax: (610) 593-2002
E-mail: Info@schifferbooks.com

For the largest selection of fine reference books on this and related subjects, please visit our web site at **www.schifferbooks.com**.
We are always looking for people to write books on new and related subjects. If you have an idea for a book please contact us at the above address.

This book may be purchased from the publisher. Include $3.95 for shipping. Please try your bookstore first. You may write for a free catalog.

In Europe, Schiffer books are distributed by
Bushwood Books
6 Marksbury Ave., Kew Gardens
Surrey TW9 4JF England
Phone: 44 (0) 20 8392-8585;
Fax: 44 (0) 20 8392-9876
E-mail: info@bushwoodbooks.co.uk
Website: www.bushwoodbooks.co.uk
Free postage in the U.K., Europe; air mail at cost.

Photo-like orange accent tiles create a border next to textured tiles every bit as dramatic in their effect.

Contents

Repeating circles unify a blend of blues.

Why Tile?

All natural: Ceramic tiles are thin slabs made from clay, silica, fluxes, coloring and other raw materials, that are ground and/or slipped, molded, dried, and then fired to render them stable. The raw materials used to make ceramic tile are from the earth and when combined with water and fire, they produce a natural, high quality product.

Easy to clean: Ceramic tile is easy to clean – a damp cloth, with or without detergent, suffices. For this reason, ceramic is used generally in bathrooms, kitchens, hospitals, laboratories, swimming pools, and factories, where their use prevents the generation of dirt and odor.

Hygienic: Ceramic repels moisture, which, in turn, prevents colonies of germs and bacteria from breeding. Some ceramic tiles have a compact structure and low porosity so dirt and grime does not collect as readily as on other surfaces.

Anti-allergenic: Ceramic almost electrically "repels" dust in the atmosphere, and because it's so easy to clean, it does not harbor the dust, dander, pollens, and other irritants associated with common allergies.

Easy maintenance: Ceramic surfaces do not require any maintenance after installation, except normal cleaning.

Durability. Ceramic tiles are resistant to abrupt temperature changes, chemical and biological agents, friction, and combustion.

Because it's just so darn good looking: Obviously you agree. You bought this book!

About Spanish Tile

Spain has been on the cutting edge of tile technology for centuries. Spain's induction into the ceramic tile manufacture came with the invasion of Arab culture in the 11th Century. Spain's first impor-

Neutral and fiery red work in exciting juxtaposition.

tant production factory was established in Malaga. In the 15th Century production was transferred from Malaga to Manises, which marked the beginning of a fruitful relation that would last for centuries between the Andalusian hub and the Mediterranean strip of the Iberian Peninsula, where the greater part of Spanish tiles are currently produced.

The use of tiled paving and stays became an extended custom in the south of Spain and designs became progressively more complex, with meticulous geometrical shapes and elaboration, as can be seen from tiles that decorate rooms of the Alhambra of Granada. In the 14th and 15th Centuries, unusual levels of sophistication were reached, fundamentally in the arabesque tiling technique used in paving and stays.

At this time, tile became an invaluable source of income and served to export the image of Spaniards and their high standard of living. Tiles from Manises and Paterna were also used in constructions in Liguria, and tiles were sent to Egypt, Syria, Turkey, and Italy. In 1445-57, Alfonso the Magnanimous ordered his palace, Castel Nuovo, in Naples, to be floored with tiles from Manises decorated with his coat-of-arms. Manises also became the central supplier of paving for the Papacy itself,

Interlocking tiles in delicious vanilla and chocolate flavors evoke a retro sensibility.

whose rooms it decorated during the 15th Century. Toward 1500, with a slump in production by Manises and Granada, other cities took over, especially Seville and Toledo. These cities were the main production centers of a new technique: the decoration of the main motif on a square piece, which greatly facilitated laying. The first mass production processes were also created, and the success was tremendous. Within a few years it had invaded the Spanish, European, and American markets. The latter specially needed a cheaper product that would allow it to be exported and above all, that would be easy to lay. Tiles from Seville also reached Great Britain, furnished the Vatican rooms of Pope Leon X (1513-1521) and the San Angelo castle in Rome, besides decorating palaces in Naples and Genoa. In the 19th Century and beginning of the 20th Century, Spanish tile manufacturers entered a proto-industrial stage that resulted in the appearance of the first printed catalogues, the incorporation of promotional aspects of the product, and the Universal Exhibition of Barcelona in 1888. Years later, technological advances would bring Spanish ceramics to the superior quality levels that it maintains today. Traditionally, tiles were manufactured almost entirely by hand. Since the seventies, tradition and automation have come together, making tile more accessible to the masses.

With technological advances in both mechanical and aesthetic properties, tile is positioned to become a material of choice for the 21st century. Improved indoor air quality, hygiene, fire resistance, easy maintenance and longevity are ceramic tile qualities that support sustainable design principles. Moreover, tile is unlimited in its diversity, be it size, shape, color, style, or texture.

Javier Soriano, ASCER foreign trade and export promotion, said, "The ceramic tile industry has been a significant part of Spain's culture and trade for hundreds of years. The quality and craftsmanship of the tile is absolutely exquisite. We're eager to share the advances we make in meeting the design needs of architects and design professionals as well as consumers in our biggest market, the U.S. We've made a commitment to aggressively communicate that Tile of Spain branded ceramics are on the cutting edge of design and technology."

Bathrooms

A tiled chair rail defines the color palette of a bath area. Bottom left: A random tile mosaic surrounds a step-down tub.

Top: A glass vanity allows a backdrop of tile to shine through. Bottom right: A red wall beckons within tile walls highlighted by mixed matte and gloss finishes. Right: A bold calico of color makes a striking bathroom design.

Left: Warm earthen tones invite one to linger in this bath. Background: Red and white tones are seductive in this large spa bath.

Top: Art Deco is recalled in a stunning black and white bath. Center: Small rectangular tiles are set at jaunty angles to form a rail within the white and wood-like tiles. Bottom: A great sink bowl finds its setting within two tonal variations of marble-like tile.

Top: Blue tones alternate in a tiled bath. Bottom: Metallic tones on a warm black ground define this spa bath.

Black and white define this ultra-modern bath. Bottom right: Tile makes for a crisp, clean bath environment. Bottom left: Blue descends waterfall-like over a sink bowl, fed by a grounded faucet.

Wheat and orange tones were paired artfully in this expansive bath. Center: An oversize clock emphasizes schedule in a bath area designed for efficiency. Bottom: Creamy tones and blue accents outline a spacious room, where an oversize tub beckons.

Right: Jade glass and tile accents add focal interest for an elegant bath. Below: Masculine effect is attained with bold strokes of black and white.

Top left: Rose and dark-wood tones team up in a lavatory alcove. Top right: Neutral tones of tile are arranged for texture in a lavatory setting. Bottom: Three sizes of rectangular tile are paired to create zones.

Right: Black and white tiles are married for striking effect. Below: Pink lilies on a lime ground are unforgettable adornments in a feminine bath.

Left: A bubbling spa beckons within a tile surround. Bottom left: A sloped sink impels one to wash, simply to see the water disappear. Bottom right: Tile backs a farm-style sink.

Top: Masculine modernity is effected with oversize tile in rich, charcoal tones. Bottom: Faux marble tiles add richness to a lavatory setting.

Green stripes add a retro effect.

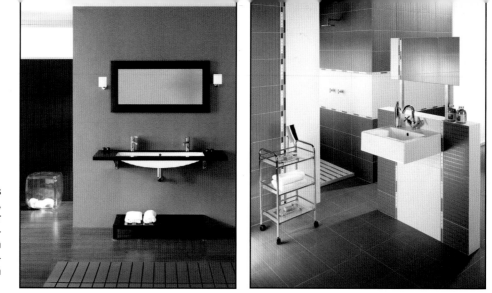

Right: Oriental aesthetics are implied in a balanced, brown-toned bath. Far right: Blue and white interlock for a dreamy clean bath. Below: Artwork accentuates the warm earth tones of a tiled bath.

Left: A gilded mirror frame and brown tiles add texture to a bath. Bottom left: Luminescent tiles create a stunning lavatory environment. Bottom right: A cream color unifies floor and walls.

Grey tones neutralize the warmth of a sun-filled bath. Below: Two tones of tile are made richer by the textures.

Top left: Gunmetal grey tile forms a backdrop for this bath. Top right: Tub and sink sit in a surround of clean tile. Bottom left: Mirrors repeat an accent tile wall.

Top: Exotica reigns in a bath dominated by a zebra rug and raised tile walls. Bottom left: Red accents could be replaced by any color du jour in this grey and white lavatory. Bottom right: Teal tile has a translucent effect, creating the feeling one is walking on water.

Tile hugs a curved wall in
this contemporary bath.

Natural tones intermingle, a tonal harlequin pattern used to add texture and definition.

An ornate frame and pedestal lamp place traditional furnishings in a contemporary bath.

Warm wood tones on cream soften this bath.

Dark tiles inset on the floor mark a passage through this bath.

White and grey tones team for a lavatory.

Hazy grey tones create a
cloud-like, dreamy atmo-
sphere.

Slate-like tile spans the wall in a contemporary powder room.

A slash of shelf spans a stretch of tiled wall.

Top: Slanted, S-shaped tiles help define and adorn borders. Top right: Two tones divide and define a bath with Asian sensibilities. Bottom right: A lounge chair and spacious tub are main attractions in a spa bath designed for lingering.

Accent tiles create a splash of color.

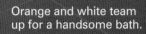
Orange and white team
up for a handsome bath.

Left: An ivy border frames a black backdrop of tile. Below: Masculine simplicity is defined in three tones.

A great round sink sits flanked by slate grey tile.

Green brings the garden indoors, infusing bright, inviting fashion.

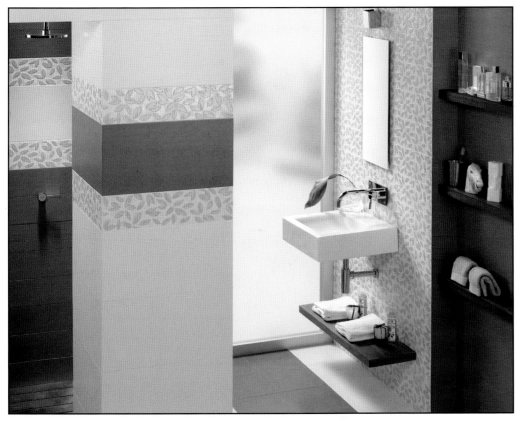

Top left: Metallic accent tiles adorn a lavatory. Top right: Asian sensibilities combine in a two-tone bath. Bottom: Slight tonal variations form a pleasing palette.

A pedestal sink and oval mirror bring old fashioned sensibilities into the bath setting.

Top left: Contemporary bathroom accouterments climb a striped tile wall. Top right: Textured tiles back a beautiful vanity. Bottom left: Futuristic in effect, a banded motif pattern plays up the wall. Bottom right: A complex interplay of color and style demonstrates great forethought.

Top: Metallic accents seem to stitch a room together. Bottom left: Black tile effects an undersea feel. Bottom right: Tile creates two horizontal slashes upon which contemporary furnishings were hung.

Dark tile unites zones within this sunny bath.

Above: Vanity and mirror take on a horizontal role, carefully affixed to a tile wall. Background: A rich, textured backdrop plays home to a contemporary vanity.

Above: Stone-like tile protects this bathroom, floor to ceiling, from moisture damage. Far left: Wainscoting is effected using tile and a decorative border, the two-tone effect lending a feeling of height to the ceiling. Left: Subtle tonal shifts adorn these walls.

A textured tile border
caps a tile vanity.
Squares are playfully
repeated in a floor motif.

Left: Bright green and blue are daring, cheering environmental additions. Bottom right: A cloud-shaped mirror floats amidst a playful arrangement of earth and sky tones. Bottom right: Tile provides earthen tones and textures.

Above: Retro squares form a barrier between black and white. Top right: Glass shelving suspends beauty supplies against a tile background. Right: Grids of square and contrasting dark and cream tones recall Japanese design.

Textured metallic blue creates zing in a powder room.

Slate grey and tan team up for a warm washroom.

Above: Blue glass vanity fixtures find a nice medium within black and white tile. Left: A stepped tile platform houses a bowl sink, offering an artful vanity.

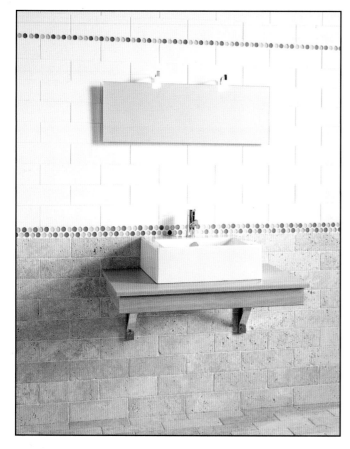

Top left: Mirror and vanity play a minimalist role against a backdrop of tile. Top right: Wood and clay tones in easy-maintenance tile create an aesthetically pleasing powder room. Bottom right: Retro flowers beat the blues in a cheerful bath underlined by bright orange. Above: A tiled platform provides a stage for long, luxurious soaks.

Multi-toned tiles in a field of blue bring
cheer to a thoughtfully furnished lavatory.

Bright blocks of
color stand in joyful
expression.

Subtle pink and lavender testify to a feminine touch.

Red, white, and black interplay behind a pedestal sink.

Tan and white work in contrast to dark wood tones in a spacious spa bath.

Lime lights up a modernist arrangement of black and white. Below: Soothing neutral tones create an atmosphere of escape. Bottom right: Natural tones create soothing effect.

Deeply soothing tones of blue unite in a spacious spa bath.

Textured tiles stacked horizontally create a curtain-like effect in the upper half of a powder room while mimicking the checkerboard on the floor.

A mosaic in golden tile brings 'bling' to the bath.

Background: Red and white interplay against a white-on-white mosaic. Above: Stone-like squares of tile, large and small, define the curvaceous boundaries of this bathroom.

Top: A brick-like wall provides a privacy screen beside a deep whirlpool tub. Left: A stylish contemporary bath setting enjoys a neutral tile environment.

Diagonal inset tiles create a visual and pedestrian tour through a stretch of spa-sized bath.

Top: A floral pattern makes a subtle statement on barrier wall and border. Bottom left: A vine border adds elegance and sophistication to a cream and blue tiled bath. Bottom right: An asymmetrical arrangment adds to the Zen-like atmosphere of a lavatory.

Bold red adds its rosy
glow to furnishings and
occupants of this spa-
cious bath.

Above: Orange provides accents for a clean white bath. Right: Blue and white provide a bright bath environment under blue steel beams.

Top left: A two-tone floor creates a shimmering bathroom surface. Top right: A grey band carries the floor color to the walls for a harmonious effect. Bottom left: Circles are repeated on rectangles in a modernist's dream. Bottom right: Horizonal bans and a leafy vine motif are used to great effect in this blue and white bath.

Right: A retro sensibility is captured in brown and white with touches of orange sherbet accent. Background: A uniform beige and cream seems to expand the space in this relatively tight bath.

Top: Vanilla tones interplay. Bottom left: Large tiles add curvaceous texture to a cool white and blue powder room. Bottom right: Masculine hard lines and steely grey tones define this spacious bath.

Right: In a minimalist presentation, this soaking bath and scant bowl sink float within a gleaming cream tile surround. Bottom left: Soothing neutrals define this powder room. Bottom right: Staggered tiles mimic a staircase in the background, within a creamy surround.

A handsome blonde vanity and broad-rimmed sink are suspended on a multi-toned tile wall.

Handsome slate grey and terracotta tones combine for a masculine, contemporary setting.

Left: Tonal grey tiles outline a shower and lavatory. Below: A backdrop of small golden tile casts a glow over a blue and white bath. Bottom: Rich dark grey and off white team up in a contemporary bath.

Top left: Sandstone-like tile provides an environment for his and hers sinks. Top right: Warm beige tones play home to red and white accents; accents that can be easily altered to satisfy a whim for change. Center: A vertical span of pretty accent tiles and impressive, stone-toned planks adds intrigue to a wall. Bottom right: A chocolate and cream checkerboard creates a base for candy-colored accents.

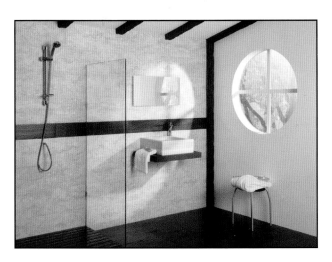

Top left: A moon window casts illumination on the tile stretch of wall backing sink and shower. Top right: Black and blue are segregated by a broken white middle ground. Bottom left: Warm brown tones bring comfort to a bath.

Above: Two floral tile patterns alternate on one wall of a pretty tan and white bath. Top right: Monument-like, two bowls perch atop tiled pedestals in this stone-toned bath. Right: Frosted panes filter natural light, and introduce a Japanese aesthetic to a clean, tiled bath.

Marble-like tiles add wispy, soft effect to tiled walls and fixtures. Bottom left: Antique mirror frames and marble-like tile imbue this room with a sense of history. Bottom right: Pink lilies and accents steel attention from a subtle green and cream environment.

Stripes give vertical lift to the tile surround of this lavatory.

Patchwork effect creates a cozy atmosphere for a vast, tiled spa.

Top: Blue and cream mix dramatically in a corner. Left: Floral accent tiles provide décor within a minimalist environment. Bottom right: Red works in stark contrast to a neutral room.

Metalic flowers flow starfish-like across a bathroom border. Background: Lavender and white provide a pretty place setting for a striking dark vanity.

Left: Ivory toned steps ascend a tiled surround to a sunken paradise. Below: Tiled walls and floor keep cleanup simple for a spacious bath area. Bottom left: A custom tiled bath is blue and white with sailors' stars above.

Top: The ultimate in minimalist, two tones of tile define the functions of a bath. Right: A spa is artfully surrounded by tile. Bottom right: Rippling sheen from glazed tiles acts as backdrop to mirrors and white lavatory fixtures. Bottom left: Lavender tones convey a playful, unisex signal with his and his, or hers and hers, facilities.

Orange and white were playfully mixed to create an eye-opening stage for the morning shower.

Above: A pretty tile border separates two attractive, neutral tones. Top left: Burnt orange, burgundy, and vanilla cream make eye candy on a shower wall. Top right: Stone-like tile tones form a smooth, inviting shower stage. Bottom right: Wood textures in natural and white form the backdrop for an artful shower.

Block tiles mimic random mosaics made of broken tiles, with far less assembly time required!

Right: Vertical accent tiles line a far wall of a spacious bath. Bottom right: Steely tones form a serene, somber place of repose and purification. Bottom left: Orange and blue offer a wildly exciting palette of color for the adventurous designer.

Above: Tile exactingly replicates wood in a spa surround, without the long-term maintenance issues. Bottom left: Orange and black create a masculine, contemporary effect. Top left: A mosaic marks a central point in a spacious spa.

Right: Orange from top to bottom has an interesting, glowing effect in a bath. Bottom left: Varying horizontal bands defy definition in a two-tone bathroom with masculine effect. Bottom center: Blue tile in two sizes provides the backdrop for a soothing shower. Bottom right: Grey and white tones interplay in a shower area.

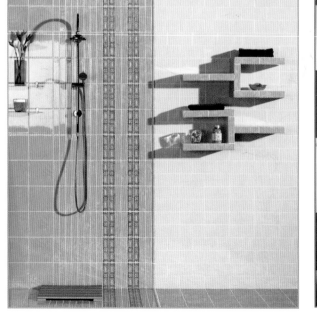

Above: Farmers' sinks cap a slash of vanity, set against a zone-defining tile wall. Top right: Contemporary furnishings adorn a steely grey tile wall. Bottom right: Brick tones mix with shades of black and white.

Kitchen and Bar

Tiles formed to portray fruit and carved molding, crowns tall tile wainscoting, capped by textured stucco.

Above: A designer played with repeating rectangles, found in textured tiles, window-panes, and cabinetry. Top: Tile mimics cut stone on center island and walls, adding texture to a contemporary kitchen. Bottom right: A Mediterannean flair for color is found in earth-toned tiles arranged on counter, backsplash, and hood.

Top: Floor and wall provide an interesting play in scale, as two sizes of tile repeat the same seemingly random pattern of neutral tones. Bottom: Tile planks add a dynamic element to the contemporary setting.

Above: A built-in work area is highlighted by a mix of terracotta-toned tiles. Top right: Tile in two sizes is used to cap a built-in shelf and cook-top area. Bottom right: Dark flooring provides a warm undertone to this contemporary kitchen.

Left: Diagonal flooring is used to add spacious effect to a room. In this case, the use of three sizes and tones of tile arranged in a parquet pattern provides one of the room's most effective ornaments, as well. Below: Playful tones make a bold statement in this breakfast nook. Bottom left: Tiles take on two roles in this room – that of neutral background, and the lead roll of ornamentation.

Right: Accent tiles encircle a kitchen carefully constructed in two contrasting tones. Bottom: Earthen tiles provide a warm setting for the family's meal preparation.

Above: A stylish blue light, a floral arrangement, and a sleek steel hood become art within the neutral tones of this kitchen setting. Top left: Tile imitates brick, while proving far easier to keep clean. Top right: Marble tones add a sense of regal timelessness.

Right: A worktable and bar tucks neatly against a wall when not in use. Below: Display cabinetry and cook-top seem magically suspended against a tile backdrop.

Left: Orange cabinetry lend their warm glow to tile flooring that mimics wood. Bottom right: Tile on floor and wall add a monumental sense to this cook area. Bottom left: A mod red motif and glassy white tiles lend their oversize presence to the walls of a stainless steel kitchen.

Large floor tiles reflect their mauve tones upward to this contemporary room.

An exciting mix of blue and sand tones adds a festive, seaside holiday feeling to this kitchen.

Blue accent tiles help define perspectives in this well-stocked bar room.

Top: Tile outlines a wonderfully-handy inset created for the tools of cooking. Right and above: Glazed tile and accent pieces lend beauty to a kitchen.

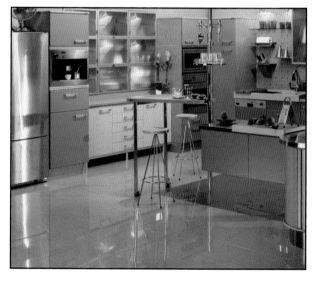

Above: Bright blue and a touch of red reflect up in the glazed finish of floor tiles. Top left: Accent shelving creates display nooks on a tile wall. Top right: Tile crowns ceiling and floor in this rustic-toned kitchen. Right: Staggered floor tiles set on the diagonal can help create a sense of more space.

A kitchen is warmed by wood and cream tones in textured tile.

A two tone wall is defined by a chair rail and an accent strip just beyond eye level.

Opposite page: Strips of tile effect warm bamboo matting on the wall, but bypass the maintenance issues. Above: A reflective tile floor serves as staging area. Top: An emphasis on storage dictated the perimeters of this kitchen. Bottom right: Tones of cream and blue harmonize.

Seaside tones unify a
kitchen and the dining
area beyond.

Left: Warm wood tones ground a country cabin. Below: An expansive floor is broken up with two patterns of tile. Bottom left: Blue flooring reflects up into a bright, cheerful kitchen.

Right: Black, granite-like tiles create a mirror-like surface. Below: A checkerboard floor forms the base for a kitchen with a playful blue and white theme.

Above: Sheer drapes and silk lighting create an interesting ambiance atop the light wood tones of a tile floor. Left: Orange sherbet tones warm a white kitchen. Top left: Though new, tile was given an aged effect, creating a timeless kitchen setting.

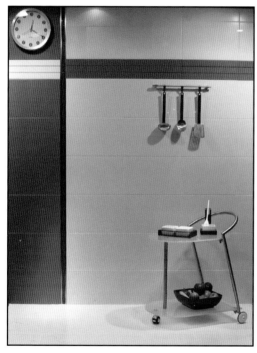

Above: Orange and white in an ultra-modern kitchen. Top left: Rustic tile were paired with stone and wood for a taste of yesteryear. Top right: Three tones are playfully mixed in size and configuration. Bottom right: Blocks of contrasting color aid the visually impaired and add stunning impact!

Left: A dedicated cook center contains the messy business of stir-frying. Bottom right: Lava tones contrast with white. Bottom left: A frosty leaf motif unifies the cool colors of this kitchen.

Right: A playful floral motif in two tones is repeated throughout a crisp white kitchen. Below: Open shelving in ultra-modern grey contrasts against a background of decorative tile.

Stone tones clad floor and walls for a cleanly, easy-to-maintain environment.

Above: Tile wainscoting is repeated in framed wall art. Top right: Lime tones lighten and brighten a kitchen. Bottom right: Earthen tones underline a steel serving counter.

Tones of green build layers along
a shiny wall and built-in display
counter.

Dining Areas

Above: Wood-like tile planks set the stage for a gallery-like living/dining area. Right: A chair rail is repeated in the floor, where the dining area is defined.

Above: A dining ledge hugs a tiled half-wall. Left: Accent tiles define a dining area. Top left: Slate-grey tiles absorb sunlight from a nearby window.

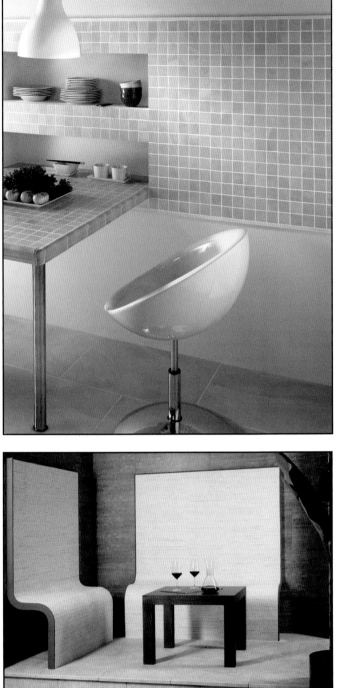

Above: A tiled environment offers a cool place to refresh oneself. Left: Red and white alternate on a wall. Top left: A mosaic floor adds elegant undertone. Top right: Tile overlays a dining counter/workspace and built-in shelving.

Above: Formal and informal dining areas share an open room, united by a black and white theme. Left: Red accents stand in striking contrast to black and white. Top left: Cobalt provides a deeply contemplative underline to a dining area diversely appointed.

Below: The elegance of black and white adorns an intimate setting. Right: Multi-toned tiles fill eye-level between orange and white. Bottom right: Natural tones intermix between the polar of black and white. Bottom left: Terracotta tones unify a great room.

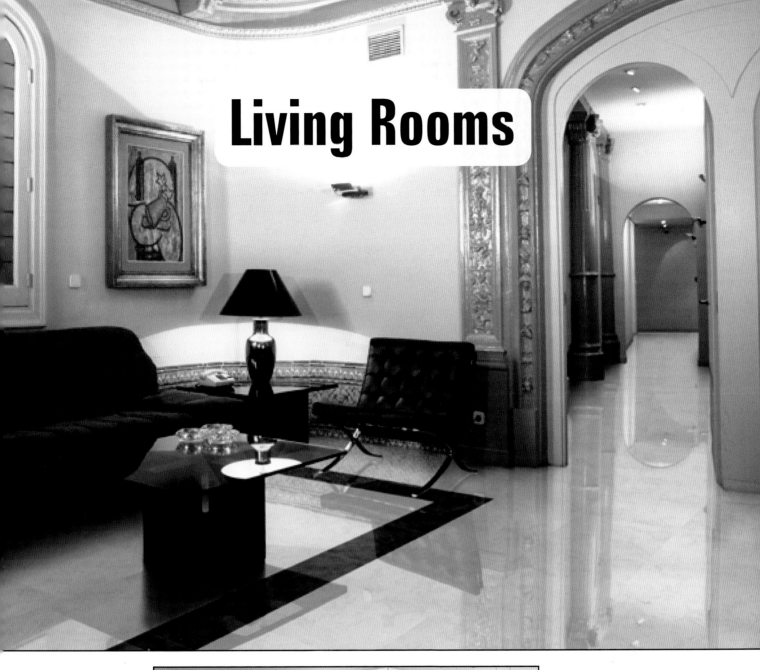

Living Rooms

Above: Incredible molded accents set this room apart, reflected in the tile floor. Left: Area rugs help define gathering spaces on an expanse of tile flooring. Indoors commingles with out in a wonderful glassed-off alcove.

Top: Creative furnishings play upon a canvas of tile. Right: Plank tiles mimic the beauty of boards while vastly improving upon the look's durability and maintenance needs.

Lower left: Neutral grey tones open a world of possibilities. Center left: Art and form display beautifully within an environment of reflective white. Top: Earthen tones underline this penthouse's connection with the natural world beyond. Right: An artist's hand playfully patterned this flowing two-tone floor.

Tile planks create the tonal richness of wood, in widths prohibitively expensive in today's lumber market. Background: Uneven edges and a tumbled look create a time-worn appearance for new tile.

Top: Contemporary furnishings display nicely in a clean tile surround. Left: An insert of wood-like tile within a lighter-colored surround creates a place of repose and meditation.

Above: Simplistic adornments and natural tones team up for an inviting space. Top right: Rich textiles, antique furnishings, and a wall mural find their place within the white setting of this room. Bottom: Oversize plank tiles downplay the spaciousness of this great room, creating comfortable zones in a series of spaces inextricably linked to the outdoors.

Above: Gradations of tone have been thoughtfully interspersed in this kitchen/dining area. Bottom left: A newly finished basement area promises easy maintenance with its tile surface. Center left: Contrasting tile helps define the boundaries in a two-level room. Top: The eye climbs from this neutral grey floor in stages, following elements of the entertainment center upward.

Above: Reflections find play within the sparkling pool of tile. Top right: Mod colors are repeated in floor, wall, and furnishings. Bottom right: This tile floor is as striking as an artisan rug, playing a key role in an owner's presentation of exotica.

Wood planking frames terracotta tiles in a wonderfully rich and rustic sunroom.

Above: Tile forms a waterfall-like wall, imbuing the room with a sense of serenity. Right: Asian aesthetics governed the furnishing of this room, including the tatami-mat like tiles.

Left: A parquet-like inset of mixed tiles forms a focal point for the room. Bottom right: A tiled wall is the focal point of this room, the fireplace shunted off to the side and reserved only for the coolest of evenings. Bottom left: Warm wood-tones are captured in a clean tile surface.

Above: A thick piled rug works as a gathering place within the expansive surround of richly-toned tile. Top right: Blocks of color and a diamond motif unify this creative space. Center right: A tiled wall and archway forms the backdrop for this contemporary setting. Bottom right: Sunny tones emphasis this room's orientation toward the sun.

Above: Crisp white, floor to ceiling, offers endless decorating possibilities. Left: A two-tiered chair rail and wainscoting in tile adds interest and texture. Top: Bold red makes a stunning statement against neutral grey.

Top: A tiled wall commands staggered heights against a backdrop of red. Center: Display shelves kept low help raise the ceiling's effect. Bottom: Tile imitates stone in a wonderful, rustic sunroom.

Fireplaces

Above: Glistening white and matte grey tile play with the theme of fire and ice in a contemporary home. Left: Tile was used to create playful "stone walls" and rich floor textures.

Above: Handsome tile work adds craftsmanship to a room with rustic appeal. Left: Deep grey tones create a sense of safe haven in this handsome space. Top left: A stretch of hearth forms an attractive perch and display area. Top right: towering tiled chimney mimics stone.

Above: Lava tones and tribal artifacts combine in this exotic hideaway. Bottom left: A beamed ceiling decorated with poster art grabs the spotlight in this room. Once one has digested this wealth of color, there's more though. Vaulted brick walls, a stone fireplace, and massive floor tiles are next in the line-up of "wow" factors. Top left: A modern slash of fireplace surround creates an exciting centerpiece for a thoughtfully furnished room.

Above: Three tile tones add ornament to the fireplace surround. Top right: Candle light provides the glow, filling a
place appointed within a steely grey slash of fire space.
Center right: An alcove mimics the fireplace, the rich tile surround forming a stone-like wall. Bottom right: Cushions pad
a tiled fireplace surround.

Bedrooms

A half-wall permits a more expansive bedroom space, eliminating a hallway.

Background: A shift in tile, though not in tone, denotes the bed's space. Center: Small tiles deliver the textural ambiance of woven reed and polished river stone. Bottom: Buffed tile magnifies the glorious light of a new day.

Top left: Smooth ceramic coats floors, walls, and the platform upon which this futon presides. Top right: A tile floor delivers the rich tones and crafted appearance of wood flooring. Bottom: While the wall between bed and bath is transparent, the rest are coated in rich tile that forms a comforting, cave-like setting for this contemporary bedroom.

Foyers, Halls, and Stairwells

Background: Flagstone tiles are arranged in an oversized herringbone pattern. Decorative tile molding along the walls adds visual appeal, and mop-proof protection. Right: Tile imitates wood with a multi-toned, herringbone design.

Left: Tile sets the stage for a hygienically cool summer room. Below: Turquoise creates a soothing, sea tone for this impressive entryway.

A grand foyer resonates with the smooth shine of porcelain.

Above: Terracotta complements wood and plaster in an inviting stair landing. Left: Tonal variations add visual impact and another level of safety. Top: Earth tones warm a contemporary room.

Floors and More

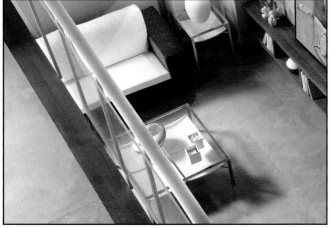

Above: Darker borders mark the perimeter of a vast expanse of tile floor. Top: A mod chrysanthemum motif and wood tones work to create harmony. Bottom right: Wonderful wood tones and a decorative border adorn a living room.

Above: Spanish style in terracotta with blue accents. Left: Tile mimics parquet flooring with pizzazz. Top: Tile unifies a series of family rooms in terracotta style, while allowing a pattern change for an inset dining area.

Two images illustrate the ability of tile to
mimic marble.

Top: Wood tones were used throughout a room to invoke nature's serenity. Bottom: A rectangular inset reflects beautifully on a spacious foyer.

Top left: Glimmering grey unites dining and cooking areas, reflecting ceiling light fixtures. Top right: Earthy purple tones reflect warmth into a white room. Above: A tumbling block pattern was used as an inset for this earthtoned entryway. Left: A mottled floor seems to dance with rippling sunlight.

...les predominate in a newly resurfaced foyer.

Interlocking terracotta tiles add art underfoot.

Above: Rich tones lend a monumental, museum-like feel to the environment of an art collector. Right: Fire, water, and air take life in the tri tones of a meditation room. Bottom right: A space undertakes the study of possibilities in black and white.

Outdoors

Above: Wood and tile cohabitate on an expansive deck. Left: Terracotta fills the voids between water and earth.

Above: Two tones and matching accent tiles were carefully laid out for an inviting pool environment. Top left: Terracotta encircles a tropical pool, the waters separated by a white line inserted for pedestrian safety. Top right: Tile caps a set of garden stairs. Bottom right: Stone and tile mix their natural tones seamlessly.

Left: Inside seems like out with a pergola-like setting established for mini-escapes during inclement weather. Below: An expansive loggia is easily maintained with a smooth tile surface. Bottom left: A screened-in area creates a picnic place, bug free.

Above: In keeping with its historic structure, a new tile surface in a loggia is multi-toned and harks back to the centuries-old art of tile laying. Top right: Tile underlines a terrace with an incredible view. Bottom right: Tile unifies an expansive courtyard space and adorns the central fountain.

A semi-circular stepped entry is kept shiny and new by its indestructible tile surface. Below: Terracotta keeps this courtyard barefoot friendly.

Top: A colorful outdoor cocina is low on maintenance thanks to the easy-clean surface of tile. Above: Natural tones floor the surface of this little balcony. Right: An incredible circular stair and loggia are crowned with tile for easy maintenance and stunning appearance.

Top left: A circular inset in a tile patio forms a focal point. Top right: Dining alfresco is ever so inviting. Bottom: A place of repose, this tiled retreat affords its visitor a sense of seclusion.

A patio area is adorned with terra-cotta and container plants.

Below: Inside and out are seamlessly unified by a tile floor surface. Right: A bird's-eye view traces the artistry of a tiled patio. Bottom right: Tile imitates stone on a narrow landing. Bottom left: An entryway impresses with a wonderful tile mosaic.

Above: An artful herringbone pattern with interspersed accent tiles captures the essence of the sea for this patio. Top left: Sun bathers find themselves at home atop the natural tones of sand. Top right: A terrace is crisply capped with tile fashioned to imitate rich marble tones. Bottom right: A tiled walkway provides an attractive entry to this home.